POWER
PUBLIC
SPEAKING

HARNESS YOUR FEAR

*40 Minutes to Master
the Top 15 Confidence
Boosting Techniques*

Michael McCarthy

www.PowerSpeakingCoach.com

ISBN 978-1-54393-688-9 eBook 978-1-54393-689-6

TABLE OF CONTENTS

READ THIS FIRST!

MY PROMISE TO YOU

WHY THIS BOOK WILL WORK FOR YOU

As the number one Stock Market Timer in the world between 1994 and 2004, I was making millions for my clients on Wall Street.

In 1998 I made one client enough money to buy the ninth largest yacht in the world.

Along with this notoriety came public speaking invitations from virtually everywhere.

I said "Yes" to almost every invitation I received.

However, when it came time for me to deliver my speech, only the scared little boy from Ellicott City, Maryland showed up at the lectern that day.

I was petrified.

I didn't know the first thing about public speaking and the audiences that came to hear me speak were expecting to be dazzled.

I had a fear greater than death.

And the story gets worse!

Every time I gave a speech, my ears would ring. I felt like I might pass out right there on the spot, and I could only hear myself in some sort of muffled, far-away voice.

My body went on autopilot.

I did not know what I was saying, had no clue if I was making any sense or not, and only knew the speech was over when I stepped away from the lectern.

It was like a bad out-of-body experience.

Before, during, and after every speech I panicked.

Oddly enough, audiences liked my public speaking.

I kept giving speeches and along the way I developed a set of coping skills— my "little bag of tricks" to stay calm.

Eventually, I began to be consciously aware of my speeches as I spoke at the lectern. I soon realized that I was blessed with having the ability to deliver a good speech.

As time went on, I began to actually enjoy public speaking.

I still use my "little bag of tricks" to this day, many years and speeches later.

It's 20 years later and now I teach public speaking.

The techniques I developed for myself are simple and effective, and I've assembled them here for you.

You won't find some of these techniques in books anywhere else because I created them.

You too can effectively use my techniques, and I offer my "little bag of tricks" to you today.

One word of advice: You need to DO the techniques to have them work for you. Simply being aware of them will not help.

It's just like diet and exercise. Knowing about healthy eating and exercise won't do a thing for you…you have to DO IT.

The good news is that the techniques are fun and easy to do.

I wrote this book for you.

You, my reader, have a gift…a story to tell the world. The world needs to hear your message…your lesson.

Fear should not hold you back.

I have the keys to help you shed your fear so you that you can share your gift with the world.

Please accept this book as my gift to you, so that you may share your gifts with the world.

Let's get started!

CHAPTER 1

Fear Is Your Friend

It's Why You're Alive Today

Come with me back in time to visit our earliest ancestors...the cave man and cave woman.

Now a tiger comes along and peeks its head into their cave.

What do you think would happen if our ancestors said, "Pretty kitty!" and tried to pet the cute tiger?

Chances are they would have been eaten alive, and you and I would not be here today.

Instead of this scenario, what typically would have happened in that cave with a fear-inducing tiger visit is the "Fight or Flight" response.

The cave man and cave woman would either have tried to run away from the tiger or tried to conquer it.

The fear response would have worked to keep them alive.

You want fear. It is your protector and it is your friend.

Yes, fear is unpleasant at best and terrifying at worst.

Public speaking triggers the Fight or Flight response.

In fact, if researchers want to create the Fight or Flight response in clinical studies, one method to do so is to tell subjects they will be asked to give an impromptu speech. It's that strong.

When confronted with public speaking, our bodies react as if a tiger is coming into our cave.

Our hearts pound, we sweat, and blood leaves our extremities to fuel larger muscles for fighting or running away, making our hands and feet cold.

It is awful. We still have a cave man and cave woman biology living in our modern-world bodies today.

But simply understanding how our bodies work and understanding that it's a protective function can help us relax.

There is no tiger entering your cave…. It might feel that way, but public speaking is not a life or death experience, and it is not life threatening.

Be grateful you have an instinctual life-preserving mechanism called fear.

And recognize that sometimes it gets triggered by mistakes in our civilized world.

It's a false alarm.

Public speaking is one of those times where we simply have a false alarm.

CHAPTER 2

Fear Is the Great Motivator

It Gets the Job Done

I am a perfectionist and I am fueled by fear. In fact, fear is like jet fuel for me.

When I was hired by Harvard University as a teaching assistant years ago, I knew something the human resources department probably did not know: I was rejected 30 years prior as a student when I applied to Harvard for the freshman class of 1984.

I said to myself, *I am not good enough to be a student at Harvard but I am good enough to help teach? Seriously?!?!*

This "secret" serves to create a low-level panic in me. I MUST do a good job. If I am "found out," I want my work performance to show that I am worthy of being employed at Harvard.

Fear makes me increase my work quality. I go the extra mile.

I treat my students like high-paying clients. They have my cell phone number and I encourage them to contact me 24 hours a day with the slightest need that they may have.

I create out-of-class supplementary workshops and seminars to advance their learning. I mentor them to the best of my ability.

My performance review ratings from the students are above average and approaching perfect.

If I had not felt "unworthy" of the teaching-assistant position and scared of being "found out" that a rejected student was now part of the assistant teaching faculty, I would not work so hard or be doing so well.

Fear is the single factor that makes me increase my work quality.

You can use this natural motivator to your advantage as well.

Like it or not, fear gets the job done.

Since fear works so well, I encourage you to see it from this angle.

Fear gets the job done!

CHAPTER 3

Reframing Fear
You Are Not Actually Afraid

The year is 2015, and I have been invited to give a speech in Kobe, Japan in 2016 to an audience of over 200 Japanese members of POWERtalk International, a group of public speakers...95 percent of whom only speak Japanese.

I'm excited! And I know about three words of Japanese.

Imagine my challenge of presenting a speech to hundreds of public speakers in a language I do not know...without an interpreter and zero understanding of the language.

The year 2016 arrives, and I am spending months, literally months, creating a PowerPoint presentation that presents my speech in the universal language of pictures.

Japan is a conservative nation with a culture very different from the United States. Being polite is incredibly important in Japan.

Every photo in my presentation is scoured for anything potentially offensive. No photos of chopsticks in rice, the number 4, or white flowers...all things to avoid in Japan.

My normally effusive body language will be toned down considerably. No yelling or jumping onstage.

No American sayings that will have no meaning in Japan. No humor or off-color jokes.

The months I spend poring over every little detail pay off.

They loved it. And they even laughed in the right places!

Now imagine if I am not concerned about doing a poor job and embarrassing myself as I prepare.

Will I put as much effort into writing my speech?

Will I put as much effort into finding the perfect pictures?

Will I put as much effort into researching the culture?

Will I put as much effort into practicing my speech?

Will I put as much effort into making contingency plans in case the PowerPoint program does not work or in case any of the many things that can go wrong, do?

Probably not.

I am not nervous, but I am concerned.

I simply really care.

Could your emotions really be concern and caring masquerading as fear?

Doing a great job in Japan was important to me, and I spent months preparing for it.

It was not fear that I was feeling, but a deep sense of caring that I would do a good job for the Japanese audience.

Next time you feel what may seem like fear about an upcoming speech, ask yourself this question: "Am I really feeling a deep sense of caring that I will do well for my audience?"

Reframing your fear as a deep feeling of caring about doing well for your audience will help you. Look at it with this lens.

CHAPTER 4

The Anatomy of Fear
Enhancing Performance

Remember that big test you had in school years ago? Go back to that memory right now.

You've studied for hours and hours for the big exam.

You've spent weeks preparing, yet you are still nervous going into the exam.

You KNOW this material.

You've reviewed it, studied it, lived with it.

You're taking the test now. You see the same questions that you studied several times.

You KNOW these answers...but you have no idea what the answers are. You have forgotten everything.

You are panicking. You do not even know where to start with an answer.

But you KNOW the answer! You studied this material a million times! You cannot believe this!

This is called "freezing" on an exam, or "blanking out."

What is really happening in the exam is your anxiety level is so high that your memory is shutting down.

This is what happens during extreme levels of stress, and it is why people forget their thoughts during speeches.

Here is a graph (courtesy of forbes.com) that visually represents the relationship between Fear (show as Stress on the graph) and levels of Performance.

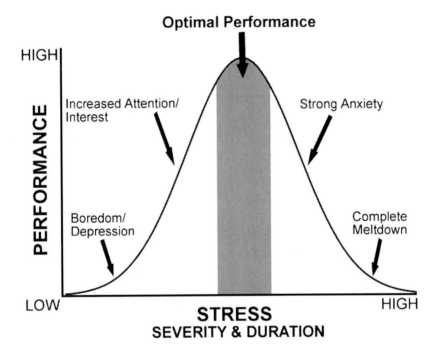

Simply stated, when we have too MUCH fear or stress, our performance DECLINES.

And when we have too LITTLE fear or stress, our performance DECLINES as well.

So what's going on?

In the public-speaking world, too much fear or stress will result in us forgetting our words, sweating, and even fainting!

Too little fear or stress will result in us not spending enough time preparing for our speeches.

If we are bored or simply do not care about the speech, our body language can be loose and weak, our vocal tone flat, and we give a pretty boring speech.

While too much fear is bad for us, so is too little.

What's the right level of fear or stress to have?

A moderate amount of fear or stress will give you optimal performance.

Having SOME fear or stress will result in you caring enough to research your speeches, practice them, and be well prepared.

Fear is your friend. You need some fear to act as a motivator and fuel you to care enough to deliver a great speech.

CHAPTER 5

Fear of Audiences

Audiences Will Not Boo...They Will Just Surf

It is the late 1990s, and I am giving a speech to a large group of Wall Street analysts in New York City, and my worst fear is about to come true.

I have been invited by the Market Technicians Association to give a presentation on how to predict stock market declines.

I am in my early 30s, and my money management firm at the time is ranked number one in the field of Stock Market Timing, the art and science of avoiding market declines.

There are over 100 professionals attending, and I am giving my speech on the 102nd floor of the World Trade Center.

This is my biggest speech to date, and I invite my parents, who are living in Baltimore, to attend.

My parents sit in the last row, the room is filled to capacity, and you can see sweeping views of Manhattan and New Jersey.

Midway through my speech I look in the back row and see my mother sleeping.

I can't believe it! My own mother is so bored by my speech she is asleep. My confidence plummets.

I look around the room and see an elderly gentleman in the front row wearing a French beret. He is sleeping as well.

My worst fear has come true. I am not giving a speech. I am giving a sleeping pill to 100 people.

What do I do?

I continue to give my speech, ignoring my sleeping mother and the man in the beret.

To make matters worse, during the question-and-answer period the man in the front row has woken up and raises his hand.

I call on him.

He launches into an attack that I have missed a key point about using interest rates to predict market declines and am therefore unqualified to be speaking.

Without missing a beat I respond, "Oh, I covered that area while you were napping."

The audience breaks out in laughter.

I am funny! I have not intended to be funny. I am just so nervous that I blurt my response out to him without thinking.

Much to my surprise, I discover that I have a new strength: Humor.

At the end of my speech, my mother apologizes for sleeping during my speech, making all the appropriate excuses of no sleep the night before, etc.

Weeks later my mother goes to the doctor about her fatigue and discovers she has a blocked artery and requires an operation to put a stent in her heart to increase her blood flow.

My mother didn't fall asleep because I was boring. She fell asleep because she had a heart condition.

And here comes your lesson: **You do not really know why your audience is behaving the way it does.**

As nervous public speakers, we assume the worst.

I thought my mother thought I was boring, but instead she was simply sick.

Avoid assuming the worst, because you might be wrong.

And audiences do not really boo unless you are incredibly offensive. If you are nervous on the stage, your audience will actually feel as awkward as you.

The worst that I have seen happen is some audience members go on their phones and read emails or texts. Even this action does not mean you are a poor public speaker. Perhaps they have an emergency.

And if someone walks out on your speech, do not assume it is because your speech is bad. Maybe they are ill or need to use the restroom. Would you prefer they stay in the room if that is the case?

Here is how to handle a poor audience: **COMPASSION.**

Yes, compassion.

Adopt a compassionate point of view when something bad happens.

If someone falls asleep, take the compassionate point of view: "Perhaps they are sick or suffer from insomnia. It is a shame they are missing my speech, but they need rest."

If someone is texting, take the compassionate point of view: "Perhaps they just received an emergency text or email. Maybe a problem has occurred at their office, their children are ill, or their spouse has had a car accident."

You simply do not know what is happening with them, and their texting may very well have nothing to do with you. Assume a compassionate point of view and wish them well.

If someone walks out of your speech, take the compassionate point of view here as well: "Perhaps they need to use the restroom, are not feeling well, need a drink of water, or are about to start a coughing fit. I am glad they are leaving to the room so as to not disturb my speech. I appreciate that."

One thing we know for sure: We do not know with 100 percent accuracy why the audience is sleeping or texting or walking out.

By taking a compassionate point of view and assuming it has nothing to do with our speech, we stay calm, carry on, and wish them well.

When this happens to you, simply wish them well.

This works for me. Try it. It will work for you.

CHAPTER 6

You Have a Gift
Focus on Your Audience

Susan was a client who came to me to calm her nerves before giving a presentation at work.

Her boss wants her to give a speech and PowerPoint presentation.

Susan is nervous. It's her first speech on this job. Her solo flight!

In the back of Susan's mind is the memory that the last presentation she gave at her former job was a disaster.

Even though that was years ago, she is still feeling nervous and unqualified.

This is not the winning mindset.

Screaming privately to herself, *GET OVER IT!* is not working.

Instead, I ask Susan to focus on her audience.

These are her coworkers. Susan knows them, and they have a good relationship.

I ask Susan to adopt the following mindset: "I know something. My boss hired me because I am good at this. And I want to pass my knowledge on to my coworkers. That's my job. I have a gift and I want to give my gift to my audience."

"Focus on THE AUDIENCE. It's not about SUSAN right now."

This simple reframing makes all the difference in the world.

Just switch the focus away from you towards them. This is key!

Anxiety and fear can only exist with inward thinking. When you are thinking about yourself (how am I feeling, I'm nervous, I'm scared) this is all ME/INWARD-focused.

By focusing OUTWARD to the audience, the anxiety goes away.

Focus on the audience. Focus on your gift. Focus on delivering your gift to your audience the best way you can.

Susan focused on delivering her presentation to her coworkers in a humble "learn-from-my-mistakes" format woven with humor.

Her focus was on relating to her colleagues.

Susan reported back that they appreciated her honesty and candor in sharing what she had learned from all of the mistakes along the way.

And they liked her casual, humorous delivery.

Susan's presentation worked because it focused on the audience.

What does your audience need to hear? And how do they need to hear it?

Next time you are worried, simply recognize that you have a gift of knowledge, wisdom, and inspiration to share.

Give that to your audience and focus on them entirely.

You will feel calm and relaxed with this point of view.

CHAPTER 7

Know Your Subject
Inside and Out!

As President of the Boston Copley Toastmasters Club (a global nonprofit public speaking organization), my goal is to ensure every attendee at every meeting does some form of public speaking.

One section of our meeting is called Table Topics, where I suggest speech topics to the audience and ask for volunteers to give one- to two-minute impromptu, off-the-cuff speeches.

I spend a lot of time creating intriguing questions, like:

"If you knew the answer would be 'yes,' what would you ask for in life?"

"If you could alter one small moment in history, what would you change, and why?"

Much to my dismay, I have very few volunteers who want to answer these questions.

Why?

Two reasons: (1) the audience is scared and (2) these are challenging philosophical questions.

When I change my tactic, and start asking memory-based questions, things change.

Examples:

"What is your favorite fun free thing to do in Boston?"

"A tourist has just arrived in Boston. Suggest something they should experience while visiting the city."

These are MEMORY questions based on a REAL-LIFE EXPERIENCE.

The participation rate skyrockets. It is easy to get volunteers now.

Why the big change?

Because when you speak from MEMORY and a REAL-LIFE EXPERIENCE, the speech is already written.

All you have to do is re-tell the event.

Since the speech content is already done, all you have to do is focus on the delivery portion of your speech: your body language, speech organization, and word choice.

It is a simpler speech to give, because all you do is describe what has already happened to you. It's easy to know what to say and what to say next. Just tell the story chronologically and describe the picture in your head.

Also, audiences want to hear from an expert who knows his or her material.

You will not look like an expert reading notes about material you are not familiar with. Audiences can tell.

If you simply give a speech about an experience you have already had, then you are the expert. You know this better than anyone else in the world, because it really happened and it really happened to you.

Giving speeches where you know the material inside and out means it is deeply ingrained in your memory. Recall will be easier.

Want to play it really safe?

Give a speech where you tell stories about your childhood, or events that occurred years ago. These are memories etched in stone. These are stories you have told hundreds of times. They will be easier to recall since they are so ingrained in you.

Your fear level will drop when you know you are giving a speech about a topic you know incredibly well, and stories of previous experiences are perfect for this.

The memory stories can illustrate lessons you want to teach, pearls of wisdom you want to give to your audience.

If I want to give a speech about the benefits of honesty, I would tell the following true story:

"I am 8 years old I want a new box of crayons for school, and my mother refuses. She says I have plenty of old crayons at home. But I want new ones for school.

"So, I shoplift a small box of crayons from the local discount store because I do not have the 25 cents to pay for them.

"I immediately feel guilty and I am scared that I will be arrested and go to jail. I go through my pockets and find 13 cents.

"Out of an abundance of guilt, I leave the 13 cents on an unattended cash register and run out of the store.

"When I bring the crayons to school I feel like a thief, because I am.

"I do not feel any pride in my drawings…because they have been created with stolen crayons. I throw the drawings in the trash at the end of class.

"I learned an important lesson. I am my own police officer, my own judge, my own jury.

"I cannot do dishonest things because I punish myself with guilt.

"Even today, as an adult, when I am tempted to do something wrong, cut a corner, take advantage, I remember that day when I stole the crayons and I remind myself...it will always be the same.

"There will be no pleasure for me from dishonesty...and that's what keeps me honest...a 25-cent box of crayons."

See how easy it is?

We all have amazing and rich experiences and can weave stories around lessons we want to convey. A story like this will be easy for you to recall and re-tell, and the audience will always remember a good story because they can create a picture in their mind.

When in doubt about what content to have in your speech, always go with an experience and simply re-tell that story through the images you see in your mind.

CHAPTER 8

Mirror, Mirror on the Wall...
Practice, Practice, Practice

I met Chris when he came to one of my workshops to get help to stop using "um" frequently in his speeches. Chris later hired me as a consultant when he was invited by the Boston Police Department to give a speech to at-risk youth on how to use mindfulness meditation to stay calm.

Chris was nervous! His greatest fear was failing to give the speech in the allotted time and failing to give the students the information they needed.

I asked Chris to practice in front of a mirror with a timer and a voice recorder.

I also asked Chris to practice his speech a minimum of 20 times. Yes, 20 times. Speeches are not that long. Twenty times is possible, and I explained to Chris that amazing speeches are made this way.

Chris became calmer, because by timing each speech, he had the speech length mastered. He was also so incredibly over-prepared that he realized on speech day that there was no more practice needed.

Chris was excited to present!

Here are the details of how you can do this as well:

First, determine the minimum and maximum length of time for your speech. Five to seven minutes are typical times for speeches.

Set your timer for six minutes. This is right in the middle.

When nervous, we sometimes talk faster. So a rehearsed six-minute speech might turn out to be five minutes when you actually present it.

Conversely, when nervous we sometimes ramble. So, a rehearsed six-minute speech might turn out to be seven minutes when you actually present it.

Why is the time important?

Three reasons:

If you are competing in speech contests, it is awful to be disqualified because of missing the time. No matter how great your speech is, it is disqualified.

If you are invited to a conference to give a speech, you will be given a time allocation. If you speak too long, you cut into the time of the speakers who present after you. If all the preceding speakers go over by a few minutes, the last speaker (the finale) may be cut from the speaker lineup because the event is over! Believe me, if you disrupt a speaker schedule you may not be invited back. When in doubt, present a little under your allocated time.

Time shifts when you are public speaking. For some people, time slows down during public speaking, and for others it speeds up. When I give a five-minute speech, it feels like 15 minutes to me. For other speakers, a five-minute speech might feel like 30 seconds. It's good to know how time shifts for you if you are ever asked to give an impromptu timed speech.

Here's the practice setup:

Find a full-length mirror with plenty of room for you to move around a little and pivot and have room for hand gestures.

Set your timer.

Voice memo record or video record with your smartphone.

Give the speech to completion each time. If you stop in the beginning or middle to make adjustments, you will not have enough practice time for the latter part of your speech. Just keep going and note changes you want to make.

Feel free to edit and change your speech.

Each sentence should support your speech and be on point. Avoid rambling.

Speak slowly.

If you rush to get all the information into your speech, the audience will only hear the rushing. They will not hear you or your content.

What if you go over time? How do you shorten your speech?

DELETE A FULL SECTION OF YOUR SPEECH.

Yes, this is the best policy. The audience will not know what they are missing. Do not worry about it.

It is much better to make one or two thoroughly explained points without rushing than cramming in three rushed points. You will lose the audience if you rush. The audience will be distracted by rushing.

This is hard to do, but my experience has shown this gets you back into the right time frame and you do not have to hurry your speech.

I am really not kidding about giving your speech 20 times. For a six-minute speech, that is only two hours of practice.

Your audience is worth this investment of time and you will feel calm, cool, and prepared.

And you will edit your speech, and it will be amazing!

CHAPTER 9

Be an Audience Member
Audio and Video Recording

When I teach Public Speaking at my workshops, one of my goals is to have the students speak as much as possible.

On the first day of class, I ask the students to give mini-speeches, just one to two minutes long, and I critique them.

I also invite the students to go around the room and give feedback to each other on the speeches they have heard.

There are three benefits from doing this:

Some of the students make astute observations that I may have missed.

When multiple students repeat the same compliment, the speaker actually starts to believe that it is a true fact and not just me, the teacher, being supportive.

When a student gives constructive feedback (stand up straighter, be mindful of filler words), the student giving feedback does not make the same error when he or she speaks.

Eureka! My students get better and faster by critiquing each other instead of me doing it. I add a huge bonus by videotaping the speeches and letting students see themselves.

There is no greater critic than yourself. Suddenly, a whole new world opens for my students.

They start to see themselves in a new light. They start to recognize strengths. They can watch their progression over the weeks, and their confidence builds. They also note things they didn't like about their speaking and become more mindful to correct those behaviors.

In the privacy of your own home or office, I encourage you to VIDEO AND AUDIO RECORD YOURSELF.

It is a huge benefit. You can now see what the audience sees.

You will definitely see something you don't like. That's normal. Change it if you do not like it.

You will also see strengths you never realized were there.

If you do not have access to a class or a public-speaking coach, videotaping yourself is a nice second.

Be kind to yourself, though. I cringe at myself when I see video. I think I talk funny. It's okay.

We are our own harshest critic. Don't worry about it. It's a learning tool and a way to grow faster.

This is worth the effort.

CHAPTER 10

The Mental Movie
My Greatest Trick

I am fascinated with the brain and its relationship to success and anxiety.

If I am in a good mental space and think about the possibilities of what I can do in business, I tend to achieve my goals.

And when I'm in a bad mental space and think about how bad things can be, I tend to get those bad things as well.

Thoughts become things.

It's really true when you think about it. Anything that was ever created started off as an idea...a picture, to be more specific.

And this is where my greatest trick was born.

After I have created the thought seeds of my speech, I practice it in my head. I make a mental movie of my speech. This is commonly referred to as visualization.

Here's how I do it: When I go to bed, I close my eyes and start the movie of my speech. It is a movie in incredible detail. I watch myself walking into the building where I will be giving my speech, looking at the speaking space, and greeting the guests as they file in.

Every detail is mapped out, and the speech I give in my movie is perfect.

Then I fall asleep.

When I wake up in the morning, before I get out of bed I repeat the process. I do the mental movie again.

I find this is the only time of day when I can spend at least five minutes of absolute solitude to practice my speech.

Do this twice a day, morning and night, before you present your speech.

I tried to figure out why this helped me so much.

Here's the two-part reason:

1. **The brain thinks in pictures, not words.** Think about this. When you recall something, do you see a picture or do you read a paragraph of text in your head? You recall a movie, is what you do.

2. **The brain believes what it sees.** Ever get tense watching a thriller movie? Your heart rate goes up and you breathe heavier. You might even sweat. But it's only TV! Logically, you know this. But the brain doesn't. The brain believes what it sees, and that is why TV and movies have an impact on us. If we were really as logical as we like to think we are, we would be pretty bored with the little moving picture in the little TV box made up of actors.

This is what we use to our advantage in public speaking:

If you visualize a perfect mental movie of your speech, your brain believes you have ALREADY GIVEN the speech perfectly.

Subconsciously, you will calm down. And why not? What's to worry about? *You already gave the speech as far as your brain is concerned.*

This is the number one technique I use to harness my fear into a great speech.

Invest in yourself and your audience and make the mental movie right before falling asleep and right before getting out of bed in the morning.

Olympic athletes use this technique to win gold medals. You can do the exact same thing.

CHAPTER 11

Hurry Up and Calm Down!

Gratitude Lists

Patricia attended one of my workshops, and her challenge was a REAL fear.

Patricia is a scientist. At her job she was asked to give a technical speech, and one of her coworkers has a reputation of attacking speakers' credibility during the question-and-answer session.

It's so bad that she has nicknamed him "the shark."

Patricia was afraid she would be the victim of a shark attack.

To make matters worse, Patricia would be speaking near the end of her conference and have to sit through the first few speakers being attacked before it was her turn in the shark tank.

This was a perfect feeding ground for Patricia's mind to turn on itself and just focus on how nervous she is feeling.

Patricia came to me for help to stay calm during this hyper-tense period.

I encouraged Patricia to write a gratitude list during the time the other speakers gave their talk.

I encouraged her to write items such as:

I'm grateful I woke up today.

I'm grateful I have the opportunity to be a presenter.

I'm grateful the guy at the coffee shop got the perfect mix of sugar and cream in my coffee today.

I'm grateful I'm married.

And on goes the list. I encouraged Patricia to continue to list things she was grateful for that were large and small.

Patricia began to calm down. She was still nervous, but she made it through her speech and she made it past the shark without a nasty question!

No shark attack!

In the few minutes of writing, your brain begins to shift. You begin to see that life is pretty good. A speech is really a pretty minor thing in the scheme of things.

Whether you win or lose, do well or not, this will not really impact your life that much. And this is when the relaxation starts to take hold.

This contest, this talk, this PowerPoint presentation does not really matter.

So many things in life just do not really matter.

Right before you go on stage, write your gratitude list, and keep writing until you are called to the podium.

This really helps with the last minute nervous jitters. And remember to have a pen and paper with you!

CHAPTER 12

The Friendly Face
Finding Support from the Audience

Speaking in front of a bunch of strangers makes any normal person nervous.

When Jane attended one of my workshops, her big fear was the audience and all those people staring at her. Where was she supposed to look?

I told Jane that she simply needed to get the audience to be a part of her team to help her give a good speech.

You can do this yourself at every speech.

Here is the three-point checklist I gave to Jane that you can use to team up with the audience to stay calm:

Find out as much as you can about your audience and cater your speech to their needs. Give this to them as a gift.

Greet as many audience members as possible at the door before you give your speech, to create a small, yet important relationship with them.

During the greeting session, identify the friendly faces that you resonate with, and before your speech ask those persons if you can look at them while you are on the stage for moral support.

If you're too shy to ask these people, that's OK. Simply identify the faces that seem friendly to you.

When you give your speech, speak to these people. That's it. It will be like having a conversation with a nice person. And since you already chatted with these people beforehand, they will be attentive.

CHAPTER 13

Help from Your Higher Power
Finding the Right Words

Before becoming a Public Speaking Coach, I have a business startup and my partner is someone I do not know very well.

As we work together and get to know each other better, I realize I really do not like him

He is verbally abusive to his wife and thinks that everyone is an idiot and that he is a god.

I cannot stand him.

I decide to end the business, lose my entire investment, and move on, to preserve my peace of mind.

There is one problem, though. I am worried about having the final conversation with my business partner.

It can be really insulting to say to someone that I cannot stand them, and that I'm willing to lose a $50,000 investment and close out a new promising business all because they make my stomach turn.

How do I communicate this message professionally and without being insulting and creating an even bigger problem?

Enter my friend Paula. Paula is a successful real estate investor in Boston worth well over $20 million, drives a Bentley convertible, and is a great businessperson. Paula has seen it all.

I invite Paula to breakfast and ask her advice on what to do.

She agrees that my peace of mind is worth more than $50,000 and I need to preserve my sanity and get away from this guy. But how?

Paula has amazing advice.

She says, "Right before the meeting, say a prayer. Say, 'God, give me the right words.'"

I try it. It works!

Somehow, some way, the right words come out of my mouth, without malice, without judgement and I say what I need to say.

My business partner understands. He is not surprised at what I say. He has actually heard it before. (I hadn't thought about that.)

As we wind the business down, he becomes kinder and gentler to his wife. He even becomes slightly likable. In hindsight, I stood up to a bully and managed to preserve his ego at the same time.

You can do this as well.

Regardless of what higher power you believe in (or not), you can use this technique.

If you do not have a higher power, consider the "best version of your future self" being your higher power. What would the best version of YOU say?

A relative or person you respect can be your higher power.

Right before you give your speech, just quietly talk to your higher power and ask "Please give me the right words."

It works. Give it a try. You may be pleasantly surprised at the calming effect this will have on you.

CHAPTER 14

Confident Brain Chemistry
The Power Pose

Amy Cuddy of Harvard Business School has made an amazing Ted Talk on the "Power Pose" that I encourage you to google.

Basically, humans have a pose that depicts dominance, power, and confidence.

It's standing with your legs wider than your hips and your arms thrust upward forming the letter "V."

We typically see this pose when people win races or dominate one another wrestling. This pose physically releases chemicals in the brain that create confidence.

Only a few minutes of standing in the Power Pose will lower stress hormones in your body and release confidence-boosting chemicals in your brain.

You may feel a little silly doing it, but it works.

Watch the Amy Cuddy video and do the pose right before a speech.

Do the Power Pose in your home before heading off to the speaking location. Once there, and a few minutes before you present, go to the restroom and strike your Power Pose.

This will feel silly. Don't worry, no one will knock on your restroom door. It is worth doing, and when you feel the confidence surge you will be hooked.

My public speaking students love this pose and we have fun doing it.

It works! Harness the power of your fear and strike a Power Pose!

CHAPTER 15

I'm Excited!
The Ultimate Reframe

Fear and excitement are very closely related.

Sometimes we can confuse the two.

Scientific studies show that when you feel fear you can shout out "I'm excited!" and your brain will reframe itself to labeling your emotion as excitement.

If you are around colleagues before a speech, avoid saying, "I'm nervous."

Instead, say, "I'm excited!"

Your brain will believe you.

I do this one every time I speak, and it is so simple it's hard to believe that it works...but it does!

Just give this one a try.

It will feel silly. It will feel ridiculous. Fine. Do it anyhow.

It literally takes two seconds. When you see the power of this simple technique, you'll be referring to it often.

And enjoy being excited!

CHAPTER 16

You're Going to Be Great!

My Pep Talk for You

Well, there you have it.

All of my "tricks of the trade."

These techniques will take you from being a zombie on the stage, having no idea what to say, to truly enjoying giving speeches.

You can now look forward to public speaking.

You can be excited to share your gifts with compassion with an audience that may be helped by your words.

All you need to do is touch one life and all of this work is worth it.

You have a gift. Please share it with the world.

And let this book help you harness your fear into a motivating energetic power that will help you help others.

The techniques work. All you have to do is DO THEM.

Knowing them isn't enough.

Understanding them isn't enough.

Believing them isn't enough.

Agreeing with them isn't enough.

THEY WILL WORK IF YOU DO THEM!!!

These new skills you have are easy to do, easy to remember, and you can take them with you anywhere.

Please use my techniques as my gift to you.

And please let me know how they work for you!

Send me an email to <u>Michael@PowerSpeakingCoach.com</u>.

I'd love to hear about your success and experiences.

Good luck and go give a great speech!

CHAPTER 17

This Book in One Page
Your Power Summary

Below are the summaries of each chapter for quick reference:

- Fear is your friend. It keeps you from being eaten by the tiger. And fear sometimes gives a false alarm, like now. See fear as a friend now.

- Fear is a motivator. It gets the job done. Let this motivation fuel help you. Fear is your motivator.

- Are you feeling fear, or do you care deeply about doing well? Reframe your feelings into caring deeply about giving a great speech.

- Optimal performance is achieved with a moderate amount of fear. Too little fear and you don't care. Too much fear and you freeze and forget. Keep it right in the middle.

- Have compassion for your audience. You do not know why they do what they do, so give them the benefit of the doubt. Take a compassionate point of view with your audience.

- You have a gift. Focus on your audience and delivering the message of your gift to them.

- Give speeches that use real-life experiences you have had and simply tell that story. You and your audience will remember it.

- Practice your speech 20 times in front of a mirror. Make sure to time it.

- Video or audio record your speeches. See what the audience sees.

- Make a mental movie of your speech before you get out of bed in the morning and right when you go to bed at night.

- Write your gratitude list right before you give your speech.

- Learn about your audience, greet them before your speech, and find your friendly face.

- Ask your Higher Power (and this can be the best version of your future self) for the right words.

- Strike your Power Pose before you give your speech.

- Reframe your fear by saying out loud, "I'm excited!"

Now that you have read the above items, DO THEM!

Good luck, and feel good about sharing your gift of wisdom and learning with the world.